How to Write Your Book:

Beginner's Guide to Learn How to Write Your Own Book

Evan Miller

The author does not take any responsibility for inaccuracies, omissions, or errors which may be found therein.

Additionally, the information in the following pages is intended only for informational purposes and should thus be thought of as universal. As befitting its nature, it is presented without assurance regarding its prolonged validity or interim quality. The author of this work is not responsible for any loss, damage, or inconvenience caused as a result of reliance on information as published on, or linked to, this book.

The author of this book has taken careful measures to share vital information about the subject. May its readers acquire the right knowledge, wisdom, inspiration, and succeed.

Table of Contents

Introduction

Congratulations on downloading this eBook and thank you for doing so.

Writing a book is an exciting adventure. However, it is also a daunting task to write a good book. If you are one of those people who have the desire to write a book but simply do not know where to start, then have no worries. *How to Write Your Book: The Beginner's Guide to Learn How to Write Your Book* will teach you how you can write a good book from scratch to finish. This book will be your best friend on your journey to becoming a book writer. The following chapters will teach you the ins and outs of writing your own book:

- Chapter 1 — talks about the basics, so that you will have a good foundation and understanding of what writing a book is really all about.

- Chapter 2 — discusses the art of making an outline for your book. An outline works as the skeleton of your book, so it is important that you learn how to outline your book properly.

- Chapter 3 — explains the actual book writing process itself from generating ideas for your book to your first draft and all the way to the completion of your book.

- Chapter 4 — reveals the best practices that you should observe to increase your chances of successfully writing a good book.

- Chapter 5 — discusses the next steps that you can consider once you have a completed manuscript. It is time to talk about getting published and marketing your book effectively.

There are plenty of books on this subject on the market, thanks again for choosing this one! Every effort was made to ensure it is full of as much useful information as possible. Please enjoy!

Chapter 1: The Basics

Why write a book?

Before we discuss the technical points of writing a book, you should first understand why you want to write a book. There are many reasons why people grab a pen and paper and end up with a completed manuscript. A book can inform people, entertain, influence, and even change people's lives. Indeed, a book can even change the world. You may want to write a fiction novel, poems, or even your own life story.

One thing that you should understand is that writing a book is an act of sharing. When you write a book, then you must be willing to open up your heart and mind to people. Now, the truth is that there are countless reasons why you may want to write a book. You might want to share a happy or even a sad experience with the world, share your expertise, inform people or entertain them, or perhaps you want to immortalize a love story that you have. People write for so many reasons, but the reasons do not really matter. Yes, you can write a book even without a reason. The important thing is that you get yourself busy and actually start writing your book.

Okay, as you can see, deciding to write a book is not really a problem. But, the question is, "Can you write a book?"

It should be noted that anyone who knows how to write can write a book. So, yes, you can write a book. However, this is not as simple as it seems; otherwise, everyone in the world would spend their time writing books. The thing is that you should know there is a difference between writing just any kind of book and writing a good book. Just about anyone can write a book in a single day, but creating a good book requires knowledge, skill, time, dedication, and practice. However, it is nonetheless doable, and you are the right person to do it.

What kind of book do you want to write?

Generally, there are two main genres of book writing: fiction and non-fiction. As you may already know, fiction refers to books that are taken from one's imagination or fantasy; they are not real. However, it is noteworthy that many fiction books are based on real-life events. Good examples of fiction books are novels and poems.

Non-fiction books are those that are real, such as biographies and autobiographies, memoirs, history and instructional books, and the like. Do not be confused, these things are just how people classify books. Instead of worrying too much about which category the book that you want to write belongs to, you should simply focus on writing your book. After all, no matter what book you write, bookstores will always have a place for it.

However, it still helps to know the kind of book that you want to write, so that you will know which kind of approach you should take. There are many ways to express the same idea. For example, if you want to share something about your life, you may write an autobiography or a memoir, but you can also do it by writing a poem or a novel. A good advice, especially for beginners, is to take the writing path that you feel most comfortable with.

How long does it take to write a book?

There is no hard and fast rule as to how long it takes to finish writing a book. Some people only take a few days, while others can take months and even years. Of course, the word count also matters. Obviously, the longer the book is, the more time it may take to write. But, it is not always about the word count. Keep in mind that quality is more important than quantity. In fact, many famous writers only write around 500-1,500 words a day just for a draft. Again, there are no rules as to the timeline for writing a book. However, it is better to follow a schedule or even small writing goals to avoid procrastinating. Indeed, many people who want to write their book have a serious problem with procrastination. The worst part is that they do not even realize that they have been procrastinating for so long to the point that they do not exert any effort to start writing their book.

One of the hardest parts of writing a book is actually taking positive actions to start writing. It is similar to someone who wants to go to the gym and exercise. Sometimes he may have thoughts about the exercises that he intends to do, but then he ends up at home lying in bed instead. The key here is to take positive actions. Once you have decided to write a book, then the next step is to stop wondering about your book and start to actually write it.

A good way to have an idea of how long it will take for you to complete your book is by making an outline. Do not worry; we will talk about the different ways of making an outline in detail in the next chapter. What you can do is to set a reasonable timeline as to how long you will think it will take you to complete the parts of your book as shown in your book outline. It is important to be reasonable. You should consider how much time you can devote to writing your book.

Now, there are writers who are too conscious about the word count for their book. However, it should be noted that it is not really that word count that matters, but the quality of your words. For example, you would rather have a 40,000-word quality book than a 100,000-word book that is full of fluff. Again, instead of focusing on the word count, focus on the quality of your writing.

As a simple rule to remember, the more time that you devote to your book, the more likely it is that you can come up with a good book and the more motivation you will get to write it faster. A common problem people face when they try to write a book is not giving it enough time. It should be noted that writing a good book is not an easy task. Just like anything that is meaningful, you need to give it plenty of time and effort.

What makes a good book?

You might be wondering, "Just what exactly makes a good book?" Technically, this will depend on the kind of book that you want to write. For example, if you want to write a novel, then you must have a grabbing plot, interesting characters, and others. If you are writing a non-fiction book, then it must be informative and easy to understand. Whether a book is good or bad may also depend on the preference of the reader. It is hard, if not impossible, to please everyone. However, you have to understand that writing a book is a solitary act. What is important is that you are happy with your book. How other people respond to your book is outside of your control. The most important thing that you should remember is that you, as the writer, should be happy with your book. This is what you should never forget as you pursue a career in writing. As long as you are happy with it, then the book is good. However, if you write a book only to earn money from it, then you will have to consider the competition, as well as market acceptance, and other factors. It should be noted that the level of competition in the book industry is tight. However, do not be discouraged as there is always an opportunity for you to reach the bestsellers list, especially if you approach book writing the right way.

Once a book gets published and reaches the market, that is where things can get complicated. This is because whether or not your book is good enough will be subject to the preferences and criticisms of other people, and this is something that you cannot control. It is also worth noting that even best-selling books have their own share of critics. Once again, do not expect that you can please everyone.

There are, of course, certain measures that you can do to increase the chances of having people to like your book, such as observing proper grammar and punctuation, getting your point across clearly yet artistically, having an interesting plot (if you are writing a novel), and others. It should also be noted that before you can say that you have written a good book or not, then you must first be able to finish writing a book, and this is what is important. Again, if you are happy with your book, then that is a good book. Now, if other people also think that you have written a good book, then consider that a big bonus.

However, if your reason for writing a book is simply to become popular and probably make money from it, then you should take a more technical and professional approach. You should study the books in the market that are similar to yours and see how your book matches up to its competitors. Having a strong following is also a big plus. After all, when it comes to generating sales from your books, then a big part of that would involve taking a business approach.

Now that you have a good understanding of what it means to write a book, it is time for you to learn the actual steps of writing a book.

Chapter 2: Outline

Book idea

Before you start writing your book, it is good to start with writing an outline for your book. Your outline will serve as the framework or skeleton of your book. Since it will be the main foundation of your book, it is important to be careful with making your outline. Take as much time as you need, and do not hurry. However, before you can start making an outline for your book, you first need to have a book idea, "Just what is it that you want to write?"

There are many sources for a book idea. It may be simply something that you feel writing about, or perhaps there is a market demand for a particular book. For example, during the time when cryptocurrencies were becoming popular, there were many books on cryptocurrencies that got published. Think of your book as a product that you will offer to the market.

Write down your ideas on a paper. Once you have different ideas written down, decide which of those ideas you would want to write about. Now, once you have an idea of the book that you want to write about, it is time to be more specific. A good way to do this is by asking yourself, "What is it about your chosen book idea that you want to write about?" These days, having a book that is too general is no longer recommended. Again, do not forget that the competition in the book industry is tight. So, for example, this book that you are reading right now is about writing, but it is not just about writing. Rather, it is a book about writing that is essentially for beginners. Hence, you should not expect for it to be too technical, but at the same time, it should convey the right and substantial information to the reader. Hence, there are two important things to remember: You have to pick a book idea, and then make it specific.

Once you are happy with your idea, try to develop or improve it further if you can. Give it some more time and do not rush into writing your book. If after a day has elapsed and you still cannot think of a better book idea or a way to develop your current book idea, then ask yourself if you still want to write the book. If the answer is yes, then it is time for you to take positive actions and start making a book outline.

What is an outline?

Think of the book outline as the framework or skeleton of your book. This is where you plan and map out the different parts of your book. It is true that there are writers who do not use an outline, especially those who are into fiction writing. However, it should be noted that many professional writers use an outline, especially those who are into non-fiction. An outline simply makes writing the book much easier and gives you a sense of direction. Hence, making an outline is strongly advised. Now, there are different ways to make an outline, but their purpose remains the same, and that is to give you a sense of direction in writing your book.

Ways to make an outline for your book

There is no right or wrong way of making an outline as long as it can help you in writing your book. The following should serve as your guide when making an outline but do not let them limit you in any way. Again, an outline should help you write your book and not the other way around.

Topics + subtopics

This is a good outlining technique to use when you want to write a non-fiction book. Outline your book by dividing it using the topics and subtopics that you want to discuss. Pay attention to the sequence of the book. When writing non-fiction, it is good to start with the basics which will serve as the foundation of your book, and then gradually make your way to more specific or detailed topics. Simply map out your book with topics and subtopics beginning from the beginning to its conclusion. This will allow you to have a bird's eye view of what your book is going to be. Feel free to develop your outline for as long as you like. Keep in mind that your book outline serves as the main foundation of your book, so write it as best as you can.

Plotting

This method of outlining works best when you write fiction. The way to do this is to follow the plot of a story. What are the parts of a story? Well, remember the

following:

- Beginning
- Rising action
- Climax
- Falling action
- Denouement

As the name already implies, 'beginning' refers to the introduction or the start of a story. This is the part where you introduce the characters, the setting, and others. It is also worth noting that the setting of a story does not just refer to the place where the story took place, but that it also refers to the time when the scenes took place. London today is very much different than it was a hundred years ago. As you can see, time is also an essential element of the setting of a story. A good advice when it comes to introducing characters is to make your characters interesting enough. Your readers should want to know more about them. Also, make sure that each character has his own personality different from the others. This is how you give each character in your story his or her own identity.

The rising action is the part of the story where the main character meets or undergoes a challenge or problem. This sets up the most interesting part of the story. Therefore, it should also be interesting enough. Otherwise, you cannot expect your readers to follow the flow of your story.

The climax is usually defined as the most interesting part of the story. It is usually the part where the main character faces a challenge head on, or it's the part where he experiences a soulful realization. There are many ways to describe the climax. Simply put, it is the most interesting part. This is what you have set up in your introduction and rising climax.

The falling action is where the story starts to settle down and relaxes just after reaching its point. There are writers who do not pay so much attention to writing the falling action and fail to realize that it is also an important part of the story. Just because you are done with the climax does not mean that your job as a writer is already done. Just as when you have reached the peak of a mountain, you also have to take efforts to walk down. The falling actions are where things are falling into the right places. It is where you make your graceful exit.

Finally, there is the "denouement," or it can simply be called as the ending of the story. Just as every story has a beginning, there is also an end. There is also what's called an 'open ending' where the writer leaves it to the reader to decide what the ending will be. Also, it is now common to find books written in a series where the ending leads to another new beginning, and this usually means following up your story with another book.

Going back to how you can use plotting as an outline for your book, you simply have to map out the story by following the plot. So, what will your beginning or introduction be? Now, make it more specific. Who will be your characters and what are their personalities? Describe them and give them a role to play in the story. Make sure that every character helps to develop the story. If you find a character that does not help to develop the story, then remove that character. Also, pay attention to the setting. Do not forget that the setting of the story refers both to the place and the time where the story happened.

Once you are done with plotting the beginning of the story, then move on to the next part which is the rising action. Keep plotting and adding details. You do not have to write long paragraphs. If you want, just write a few words or a single sentence. The key here is to simply give you an idea or a sense of direction once you finally write down the book. Continue this process until you finish plotting the ending of the story. Once you are done with making this outline, you will already have a complete story in your mind. You simply have to follow your outline and fill in the details.

Chapter outline

Whether you are writing fiction or non-fiction, making a chapter outline can help you greatly. In fact, this technique is one of the most recommended ways to make an outline. When you use this approach, you will divide your book per chapter. You will then map out every chapter of the book. You do not have to write long paragraphs; if you want, you can simply write in bullet form. The important thing is to map out what will happen per chapter.

Here is a simple example:

- X meets Z in a bar
- Z leaves the bar after receiving a call from a friend
- X follows Z to her car

And so on...

As you can see, it is like plotting the story in the simplest way possible. The important thing is that you should write the flow of the story. Do not worry about the details yet, you can add the details when you finally write your book.

Character Outline

Character outline is normally just a part of any other outline. However, there are writers who are already satisfied with just making a character outline. If you are the type who wants to be led by the characters as you write the story without knowing how the story will unfold, then this may be the approach that you should learn. Making a character outline is easy. Just list down all your characters, and then describe them, one by one. Make the descriptions as detailed as possible. Do not just describe your characters in terms of appearance, but you should also describe how they think or behave. Once you have outlined all your characters, then you are done. All that you need to do is to proceed with writing the book by allowing your characters to act out on their own and lead you through the story.

This outlining technique is not for everyone. In fact, if you are just starting out, then you might not even understand exactly how all of this is supposed to work. However, some beginners like this approach as it gives them flexibility. The key here is to let your imaginative mind take over and write the story for you through the different characters that you have. After all, in any good story, it is the characters who should develop the story and not the background narratives that you make.

Should you always stick to your outline?

Okay, now that you have an outline, the question is, "Is it important that you stick to your outline?" It should be noted that not all writers share the same view on this matter. There are writers who swear by their outline while others like to be more flexible and open to changes. Take note that you are not required to follow your outline. However, just make sure that if you do not follow it, then you should be taking a better direction. What you can do is to change or modify your outline. This way you can be sure that your story will still have a sense of direction in the future. A common mistake is to abandon your outline because of a single scene that you suddenly thought about only to find out that just because of that scene, you will have to abandon the outline that you have made. Of course, this will depend on how much that scene will have an impact on the story. The point here is to be careful with not following your outline as it may get you lost in your own thoughts. Think of your outline as the signs in the forest that lead you to your destination. If you decide not to follow a sign, then just be sure that you have a good reason for it.

However, it is also not good to be too strict with following an outline as it might be an obstacle to the expression of your creative mind. Normally, when you just think of a story, your ideas will be limited. It is like a journey to an island by boat. Since you are still far away from the island, you have a limited view and ideas about what's on it. However, as you journey and get nearer to that island, the more you can see it, and the more ideas you canhave. This is also how writing a book is. In the beginning, you may only have a vague outline or idea of what your story is going to be. But, as you write your book, you get to become more inspired and receive more wonderful ideas that you can add to your book.

So, whether or not you want to stick to your outline all the time is a matter of personal preference. After all, there are no strict rules when it comes to writing a book. There is always enough space for you to exercise your creativity. As a rule, stick to your outline unless you come up with a better idea.

Chapter 3: Book Writing

The first draft

Once you have your outline ready, then you can start writing your book. Which means it's also time for you to write your first draft. This is your first attempt at writing your book. The first draft does not need to be perfect yet. What is important is that you finally start writing your book. So, look at the first part of your outline and start writing. As the term implies, you can expect to have another draft. In fact, it is not uncommon for a book to have multiple drafts before the final manuscript is completed.

Writing your first draft is important as it is what actually commences the formal journey of writing your book. As the saying goes, "The journey of a thousand miles begins with a single step." Your first draft is your first step in your journey to write a book.

There are writers who are very careful even with their first draft, but there are also people who are not as careful when it comes to writing it. If you want to avoid having to edit your draft many times, then it is good to be careful with crafting even if it's just the first draft of the book. Remember that a good book is not just about giving information or telling a story, but doing it so effectively in such a way that it will grab the interest and attention of the readers.

Revisions

When writing a book, it can be hard to avoid doing revisions. Do not be lazy. Exert every effort that you can to improve your book. This may involve having to rewrite a whole scene or even an entire chapter. Change is okay as long as it will make your book better.

You should take as much time as you need to revise your work. Revising one's work is the way to improve your writing. Remember that writing is both a skill and an art. There are many ways to express the same thought or idea. By revising your work, you can come up with better ways of expression.

Many times, while you are writing your book, you will find parts that you can still enhance. Do not hesitate to make changes. Sometimes you do not really have to change what happens in a story or a particular scene. You simply have to change certain words or phrases that will give the story a nice flow. You will find that certain words mix well and help make your story more readable.

When exactly do you revise your work? There is no strict rule as to when you should revise your work. There are writers who revise their work as they write, and there are also those who will only look for revisions once the first draft of the manuscript is done. On the one hand, the advantage of revising your work as you write is that you get to come up with a high quality of work right away. This can also decrease the chances of doing more drafts or revisions in the future. The drawback is that you may find it hard to stick with your outline. Hence, there is a risk that you might get lost along the way and not know what to write next. On the other hand, revising your work only after making a draft of the whole book will allow you to stick to your outline. However, the drawback is that you might miss out on some interesting changes or modifications in the process of developing the book. As you can see, there are benefits and consequences regardless of when you decide to make revisions.

To decrease the number of revisions that you might make, then you should be careful with writing your draft. Yes, just because you are only writing a draft does not mean that you should not pay attention to your writing. Take note that a big chunk of that draft will be put in the final manuscript. Hence, do not take writing lightly even if it's just the first draft.

Do not be surprised if you find so many parts of your manuscript that you can revise and develop. That is normal. In fact, it would be quite strange if you cannot find parts in the book that you can revise. Anything you write is subject to a revision and can always be improved. This will also depend on your skill and experience as a writer. The more skillful and experienced you are, then the more ways you can come up with to improve your draft.

So, just how many drafts and revisions should you write? Well, there is no limit to how many drafts or revisions you should make. As long as you can improve or develop your book, then do it. Feel free to revise your book as many times as you want until you are happy and content with it.

It is important for you to be honest. Some people ignore it even if they feel that they can still make some positive changes to their book. Do not be lazy. Keep in mind that the more that you revise your work, the better the book becomes.

Revising your work can take days. In fact, it is advised that before you look for things to revise in your book, you should take at least a day off without looking at what you have written. This will allow you to see your work with a fresh perspective. Just like other parts of writing a book, you should not rush the process of revising your work.

Editing

Always edit your work and do it multiple times. Editing is very important. Even if you think that you are a really good writer who does not commit any spelling or grammar mistakes, you should still edit your work several times. The truth is that it is easy to commit even the simplest of mistakes when writing a book. After all, you will be writing thousands of words. And, since you are more focused on the storyline (in case of fiction) or on sharing information (in case of non-fiction), it will be easy for you to commit some mistakes. Do not worry, this is completely normal. This is why writers hire editors. Now, if you do not want to hire an editor, you can edit your own work. However, it is important that you view your work with fresh eyes or from a clear perspective. The best way to do it is to take some time off. Stop writing and relax and enjoy yourself, so that when you go back to read your work later on, you will read it as if it was your first time seeing it. This will allow you to see it with an open mind. The problem with editing your own work is that you are not certain if other people will also understand your writing like the way you do. This is why you have to give yourself some time to review your work. Since you already know what you have written, it is easy to assume that the message will also be clearly delivered to other people. By giving yourself time to forget about the book for a while and reading it only after taking a break, you can scrutinize the book without any prejudice or bias.

Editing is important. You will be surprised how you can commit a simple mistake. This is because as a writer, you are more focused on telling the story instead of worrying about the rules of grammar and punctuation. Hence, do not be surprised even if you violate simple rules, as this is very much expected.

Editing your work means more than just correcting your grammar and punctuation. Editing can also take the form of revision in the sense that it could completely remove a scene from the story. Experts suggest that you should be heartless when it comes to editing. When you write, it is good to let your heart out and even not worry about any basic rules in writing. However, when you reach the point where you need to edit your work, then you should use your brain. Do not hesitate to remove the parts of the story that do not develop it in any way. This is another reason why writers hire editors. It is not uncommon for a writer to get attached to his writings so much he would not want any part of it to be removed from the book. It is not rare for professional writers to remove more than 2,000 words from the book once they edit it. When editing your own work, sometimes it helps to pretend that you are editing another person's work to make it easier.

Formatting

Once you are happy with your manuscript, it is time to format it. How you format your manuscript would depend on your publisher's guidelines. Sometimes it is even the publisher who would do the formatting for you. If you are going to self-publish your work and post it on online bookstores like Amazon, then you have to follow the guidelines given by your publishing platform.

Formatting can give you a headache, especially if you do not know so much about making page breaks and bookmarks, but all these things can be learned. There is no one way to format a book, so just follow the guidelines given by your publisher or the publishing platform that you are using. These days, there are many platforms for indie authors that will do the job of formatting the book for you. All you need to do is to observe their easy-to-follow guidelines, and they will do more than half of the work of formatting.

Formatting is important as it improves the readability of your work. Even if you have written an excellent book, people may not find it interesting if it is too hard to read. If you intend to publish an eBook, then all the more reason for you to learn how to format your work properly to make it compatible with different devices.

Book cover

Make sure that your book has an attractive and grabbing cover. If you are aware of the saying, "Do not judge the book by its cover," then it is time for you to know that it does not apply in the real-world market because people do judge books by their cover. Keep in mind that the competition in the market is tight. Also, before anyone gets to read the magnificent lines you have written or that amazing plot you have made, they will first see only the cover of your book. From there, only then will they decide if they still want to read further. Now, if you do not have a catchy and attractive book cover, you cannot expect people to even pay attention to your book.

Now, you can make your own book cover. But, if you are really serious about your book, it is strongly advised that you hire a professional to do it. Still, you can take the effort and learn how to make attractive book covers. When it comes to using images, use your own unique image. In case you want to use another person's image, be sure that it is part of the public domain. If not, then you have to get the permission from the person who owns it. There are also many premium images that you can purchase online. Hiring a professional to make your book cover can make a big difference. However, it should also be noted that there are many indie writers out there who make their own covers and are successful with it. The point here is to make your book cover as beautiful as possible. Yes, your book cover matters a lot.

Your cover also acts as a way of promoting your book. When you have an attractive book cover, people will want to know more about it. This is how you can persuade them to take a look at your writing and read more.

Another important thing about a book cover is your back cover. Make sure to write compelling content at the back of your book. Make the synopsis of your book interesting enough that people would want to read the whole book. Of course, do not just rely on the back cover to promote your book. The key is to also write a more compelling content in the book itself. Think of your front and back covers as something to grab people's attention to let them have a peek into your writing. But don't forget that the contents of your book must be a satisfying read.

Chapter 4: Best Practices

Time management

How you manage your writing time with other things that you do in life matters a lot. If you are one of the many who also needs to work to earn a living and only have a limited time to work on your book, then you should learn to manage your time effectively so that you can still make time for writing your book. Otherwise, you might end up just wondering about writing your book without actually taking positive actions to turn that dream book into a reality. Indeed, it is very easy to have and make excuses for why you cannot write your book. You can be busy with work, with school, family matters, and others. You have to realize that even if you have a strong will to write your book, but if you do not have time to do so, then there is nothing that you can do. Remember that time is an essential element when it comes to writing your book. You have to make time to write your book.

There are many well-known authors who once had busy day jobs. So, how were they able to write their masterpiece despite their busy schedule? Well, they simply made time for it. This is also what you should do. Some writers wake up early in the morning and get about an hour or two just to write their book before going to work. Others do it in the evening just before going to bed. There are also those who write on their phones while they are commuting to work. Of course, there are also the lucky ones who do not have to do anything else but focus on writing their book, but an opportunity like this is not available to everyone. So, if you are one of those people who can write your book without having to worry about other responsibilities, then consider yourself lucky.

If you have a busy schedule, then try to jot down on a paper how you usually spend your day and check when you have the time to write. Again, if this seems hard to do, then make time for it. This means that you will have to make a sacrifice like cutting an hour from your sleep so that you can use it for writing your book. Or, if you want, make your writing time the first priority in your schedule and jot it down ahead of all the other things that are a part of your daily routine. There is no hard and fast rule on how you can make time to write your book. The important thing is that you should take action to make sure you have enough time, and you should use that time to write your book. It is unfortunate that many people have wonderful ideas and stories in their minds, but they do not make time to write and share them with the world. Remember that writing a book is a serious and exciting journey. Indeed, it deserves to be given your time and effort.

Correct grammar and punctuation

You should use correct grammar and punctuation. Of course, as a writer, you should at least have mastery of the basics of writing. People will find it hard to take your work seriously if they see so many errors in terms of grammar and punctuation. When writing a book, it is hard, if not impossible, not to commit this mistake, and this is why you have to edit your work several times before you publish it. It is hard to come up with a book that is totally free from any grammar mistakes. In fact, many of the best books out there also have grammar mistakes. But, just avoid committing so many mistakes. A few mistakes are still forgivable and bearable, but when it gets too much, then your readers might find your book annoying to read. So, be sure to know at least the basic rules of grammar and punctuation before you even write your book.

Proper format

As we have already discussed, having your book properly formatted is important. But, what is the right format? Of course, you can follow the basic format like dividing your story using chapters and writing in paragraphs, but you should also consider the right format in relation to the reading experience that you want to share with your readers. One thing that you should know is that there is a difference between reading a paperback book and an eBook that you read on your mobile phone, computer, or tablet. If you intend to publish your work as an eBook, many writers suggest that you should divide long paragraphs into shorter paragraphs. When you use an electronic device and see a long paragraph, it can be intimidating and hard to read. Hence, it is suggested that if you only intend to publish your work as an ebook, then use short paragraphs. The white spaces will make your writing more presentable and easy on the eyes.

Now, if you intend to publish your work as a paperback copy, then you can use long paragraphs if you want. Of course, you can still use long paragraphs even when publishing your work as an ebook, but studies show that when people read eBooks, they would prefer reading shorter paragraphs than a whole big chunk or block of words. Again, this is a matter of personal preference, but it is good that you know how reading an eBook and the traditional book may have some slight differences.

Develop the craft

Writing is a craft. Indeed, you can have an idea ofwhat writing is by reading books about it, but you cannot actually learn it unless you experience the act of writing itself. In fact, even if you know all the rules and techniques in writing, it would not be enough to make you a good writer. This is because writing is a craft, it is an art that you develop and master.

Once you know how to write, then you have to develop it. The thing is that there are different ways to write about the same thing. This is what makes writing a craft. You have to learn how to make the words flow smoothly and beautifully. Take note that this does not mean using strange or complicated words that only a few people know the meaning of. Rather, it is about using simple words but presenting them gracefully.

If you are writing fiction, then you should learn how to present your characters effectively and make them interesting enough for your readers. You should not only know about the different parts of a plot, but you must also create your own compelling plot, and express it with words that invoke the interest of the reader. This is because true writing is a craft. It is not something where you just write whatever is in your mind. You have to consider your readers and give them the best experience possible.

It is suggested that you attend writing workshops and seminars. If you can, form a group of friends who are also into writing. There are also many online groups and forums where you can meet people who share the same interest and passion in writing. You can also learn from them. If you know any writing clubs or organizations where you live, then you might want to join them so you will have more opportunity to grow as a writer.

Compelling sales page

You need to have a compelling sales page. A sales page is what a potential buyer reads when he or she views your book online. Think of it as the synopsis of the book with a sales touch. Simply put, your sales page needs to sell your book.

However, do not try too hard to the point that a reader would feel that you are trying to force him or her to buy your book. Rather, be persuasive in an indirect way. Do not tell your potential buyers to buy your book but make them feel that they want and need to get a copy of your book. You might want to learn some copywriting skills before you write your sales page.

These days, many writers suggest that you should make your sales page a bit longer than the usual. Take note that this is different from your book's back cover. It is like the back cover of your book, but it's longer and has a more persuasive style enough to compel anyone who reads your sales page to hit the buy button and get a copy of your book.

The key to writing a good sales page is not to directly tell your reader to buy your book. Rather, it should highlight what a person will learn when he reads your book. Therefore, your book must have excellent contents. Just like the cover of your book, your sales page only helps to sell the book. It is still the contents of your book that primarily matter. Still, having a well-written sales page is important. Otherwise, people might not be interested at all in reading your book.

When you use a sales page, it is also suggested that you use a bullet list of the essential features of your book. Of course, if you are writing a fiction book, then you won't need to make a list. Instead, you need to write a very compelling synopsis of your story. The idea is to sell your book in a way that a reader will want to read your book.

Keep on writing

The best way to improve and grow as a writer is to simply keep on writing. As a writer, that is what you should do, write. The more that you write, the better you become. It is not a secret that most well-known authors do not become successful on their first book, not even on their second book. On average, famous authors achieve their great success on their third or even fifth book. But, of course, there are also writers out there are who lucky and good enough to establish worldwide popularity on their first book. The key here is to just keep on writing. If your first book fails to generate a decent amount of sales, then write another one. The more you write, the more you learn. The more that you learn, the higher your chances are of reaching success. However, it is also worth noting that the real success of a book should not be measured by its sales rank or the amount of money it can generate. If you come to think about it, just the fact that you can write a book is already a big success in itself.

You have to focus on the quality of your writing. There are some writers who try to measure their development in terms of word count. This is a wrong approach. If you measure your development in terms of word count, then you only measure the improvement in terms of typing speed. Do not forget that even the top-notched writers out there only produce around 500-2000 words in a day, and this is still an unedited work. Writing is a craft, it is an art. How you combine the words and give them a fine and smooth flow are also important.

Take a break and have fun

Writing a book can be so much fun. However, it can also be tiring, especially in the long run. So, take some time off and have fun from time to time. Also, writing a book is a long journey. By giving yourself enough time to relax and clear your mind, then the more effective you can be as a writer. It is also not a good idea to force yourself to write when you are already tired.

When you take a break, do not be like the others who still think about their book. This is not the time for you to do any kind of work. Instead, when you take a break, you should not even think about your book. Do not worry, after you take a break, you are expected to work on your book even more.

You should also have fun. It is not good to write your book when you are stressed out and sad unless a depressing life or emotion is the subject of your book. Although writing a book is a serious undertaking, you shouldn't forget to enjoy the process.

Chapter 5: The Next Steps...

Getting your book published

Once you have a completed manuscript, the next step is having your work published. Now, it should be noted that publishing is quite challenging. When you write your book, sometimes the passion that you have for writing is enough. However, once you venture into publishing, then there is now the business aspect that you have to consider. You need to be persuasive enough to convince publishers that your book will sell in the market. Now, this can get complicated as you also have to consider other books in your niche, as well as the level of competition.

There are two things you can do to get your book published: You can look for a publisher who will publish your work, which may be with or without cost, or you can simply self-publish your work. These days, many writers take the self-publishing route. However, it should be noted that self-publishing your work can also be very challenging.

So, should you submit your work to traditional publishers or should you just self-publish your work? This is a question that beginning writers always ask. The truth is that no option is better than the other. They have their own pros and cons. Let us take a look at them one by one:

The difficulty of getting published

When you approach traditional publishers, getting published can be a really daunting task. In fact, many bestselling books received several rejections before they even found a publishing home. This is because literary agents and publishers are very cautious of the books that they publish. And many times, they do not know which books will actually sell, so they miss out on good books. Being the writer of your book, you would not want to depend on other people whether or not your book will be published or not. Hence, if you want to ensure that your work will be published, then perhaps you will enjoy the self-publishing route. It is very easy to self-publish your work and have it distributed on Amazon, Apple store, and other bookstores. In fact, you can also sell a paperback copy of your book. Thanks to modern technology, it is now very easy to publish your book and offer it for sale (or even for free) to the whole world. This is one of the best advantages of self-publishing.

Marketing

A good book cannot be expected to generate lots of readership and sales unless it is promoted. In fact, even those writers who are already famous still continuously promote their works. This is because marketing has an essential part to play in the success of your book. Again, once you publish your work, you have to start taking a business approach. As you may already know, marketing is an important part of the business. This is why you need to market your work, especially when you choose to self-publish your work. When you become an indie author, you alone are responsible for marketing your book.

If you get published by a traditional publisher, you still need to exert plenty of effort to promote your book. The advantage here is that your publisher will also help you market your book. And since a publisher functions as a business, you can rest assured that there is already a network or audience for your book. Of course, this may not be enough, so you still need to do your own marketing efforts.

Control

If you choose the self-publishing route, then you have full control of everything: price, book distribution, marketing, and others. You are responsible for everything. Now, this is not really a bad thing. There are many writers out there who consider it an advantage that they have full control over their book. When you work with a publisher, you will have less control of your book. In fact, there are publishers that may even ask you to change your book title, or they may even ask you to change some parts of your book. In other words, although you will have fewer responsibilities, in exchange you won't have full control over your own book.

Royalty

If you work with a publisher, you won't receive the full amount of your entitled royalties, since it will be divided between you and the publisher. If you also work with a book agent, then the book agent will have his or her share in the royalties. However, in exchange, you have to support your publisher and your book agent. They will help immensely, especially in marketing your book.

Now, if you choose the self-publishing route, you can receive the full amount of the royalties entitled to you. You do not have to give a share to a publisher or agent.

Upfront fee

One of the best things about having a publisher is that there are publishers that will give you an upfront fee for publishing your work. Now, this is not always how it works. If you are a new writer, you should not expect to get any upfront payment. Also, not all publishers give out upfront fees, so do not rely on this at all as it is does not happen all the time. Still, if you meet a publisher who is willing to give you an upfront fee, then this is a big plus.

Reputation

Since self-publishing is very easy to do these days, people do not take indie authors seriously unless you are already a successful author. This is also why self-publishing has been called by some as 'vain publishing.' This is because even those who do not really know how to write can also self-publish their work. However, if you work with a publisher, it means that your work has met the publisher's standard, and so people will tend to respect you right away. This is true especially if you get published by well-established publishers like Penguin and Harper and Collins.

So, should you self-publish your work?

This is something that only you can decide. There are authors who are successful with self-publishing, as well as those who work with a traditional publisher. You may want to try both and then you can decide from there. Many authors advise that if you want to take the self-publishing route, then be sure that you have a good following. Otherwise, it would be hard to promote or market your book. So, it is time for you to be active on social media or you can come up with your own website or blog. These days, writers are more open to their readers. Even if you intend to work only with a traditional publisher, it still helps if you have your own website or blog. Even known writers these days have their own personal website.

Again, whether you should self-publish your work or not is something that you should decide for yourself. If you want to exercise full control over your book and if you are willing to handle all responsibilities, then perhaps you will enjoy self-publishing your work. However, if you want to do it the traditional way and get some support from a publisher, then you should consider working with a publisher.

Marketing your book

Marketing your book is very important. Even if you come up with a wonderful book, nobody will be able to read it if you do not take the efforts to market it. Marketing is about making the world know about your book. Another important part of marketing is positioning yourself and/or your book in the minds of the people. So, how do you market your book?

There are many ways to market your book. If you publish your book with a traditional publisher, then your publisher will most likely help you with marketing. However, regardless how you publish your work, take note that you, as the writer, will always have to exert plenty of effort to market your book.

As an author, it is your job to establish a following, be it on social media and/or on your website or blog. Indeed, if you take notice, you will see that even the most famous authors like Nicholas Sparks and Paulo Coelho have an online presence. A common mistake is to work on building a following only after writing your book. Take note that it takes time and effort to build your own network of followers. Hence, it is strongly suggested that if you have not started building a following or fan base yet, then now is the time for you to start connecting with people online, especially on social media. It is time for you to make your presence known and build a strong, high-quality network.

It is also strongly suggested that you start working on your website or blog. Also, do not use those free websites that you find online without their own domain name. Do not worry about the costs, web hosting is cheap and would not cost you more than $25 annually. It is well worth it if you want to build your name as an author.

Needless to say, what you put on your website or blog also matters.

Many writers suggest that you should combine the power of both social media and blogging. Indeed, this is the key to creating a huge following. Why do you need to have a huge following? Well, just imagine what it can do once you promote your book. If you have a huge following, all that you need to do is to post something about your book, and your followers, especially those who like you, will not just be notified that you have written a book, but they will most likely share the news about your book with their own network of friends and connections. This is how random content becomes viral on the internet. Needless to say, you should ensure that your book is decent enough that people will enjoy reading it.

If you self-publish your work, then it is a must that you take serious efforts to market your book. As an indie author, although you exercise control over everything, you are also responsible for everything. As early as now, you should do your best to connect with as many people as possible and build your fan base. Again, this will take time, so you should start as early as possible.

Beware of the most common mistake committed by so many writers when they market their book, especially when they use social media: Spending more time with marketing than writing. Indeed, it is very easy to be caught up with social media that you do not notice the time pass you by. To avoid this, you should give a limitation as to how much time you spend on social media, as well as other things that you do to market your book. Also, avoid making it too obvious that you are building a network of connections for your book. People will not like it if they feel that you only want to use them. Instead, enjoy the very experience of being open to and connecting with people. Last but not the least, do not forget that marketing your book alone is not enough to achieve success, the content being marketed, which is your book, should do the final talking and convince people that it is a good book.

Another important part of marketing is getting good reviews. This is something that you should not ignore. The moment you publish your book, especially if you are an indie author, you should start getting reviews right away. Now, there are many ways to do this. The suggested method is to send your book to a reviewer and have him or her review your book. Usually, you will have to give them a free copy of your book and even pay them for taking the time to read and review your book. There are also authors who pay people to write positive reviews about their book. Take note that Amazon does not like fake reviews, so do not cheat. Ideally, your book should be rated with a least 4 stars, 5 stars being the highest. Hence, if you can make it five stars, then the better.

You might also want to give out free copies of your books. It is not uncommon for writers to list their books for free on Amazon and other bookstores. They use these free books to gain readership and to promote their other books. Indeed, people love free stuff. By offering your book for free, you won't just promote your other books, but you can also tap a wider network of people. If people like how you write, then chances are that they will connect with you and even look at your other works. Therefore, just because you are offering a free book does not mean that you should not be careful with your writing. As a writer, you should always be careful with your writing. If you want, you can first offer a book for a particular price, and then once you have a new book, then you can offer your old book for free. This way you can also promote your new book. Many writers use this approach for a good reason, it works.

Make money with your book

Of course, it is true that many people who publish books also want to make money from their books. In fact, there are those who write books for the sole purpose of making money. Although many writers agree that money should not be your primary reason for writing a book, it is true that you can also earn an income by writing books. In fact, popular writers like Nicholas Sparks, Stephen King, Neil Gaiman, and others, have become very wealthy because of their books. So, yes, although it is not easy to make money as an author, it is nonetheless still possible, and there are many good writers who are doing it. So, do not lose hope and keep on writing until the day you publish your own book.

Ask yourself: "How much do you reasonably expect from your book?" You should know that whatever you want is doable. However, you have to take the time and effort to write a really good book. Still, do not forget that unlike other jobs or careers, money should not be the measure of your success as a writer. Of course, it will still be a big plus if you earn millions of dollars' worth of profits by writing books.

On success

How do you know if your book is successful? Well, the word "success" can be tricky when it comes to writing a book. The truth is that success is not always measured by money. In fact, there are authors out there who offer some of their books for free (normally as a part of marketing). And, even though these books themselves do not generate income or even fail to make people buy their other works, these free books can still be considered a success because it adds to their fame.

The important thing is that you are happy with your book. Now, regarding other people, this is something that is outside of your control. After all, a true writer does not write to please other people. Just the fact that you finished writing your book is already a success in itself. Of course, if people are pleased with your writing and you also earn a decent amount of money from your book, then that would be great. Still, the success of a book should not be measured in terms of money. Only you, as the writer, can tell if it is a success or not. Many authors think a book is successful if you grow while writing it. When a book creates positive change in you, that makes it really powerful and special. Of course, if it influences others in a positive way, then that would make it even more meaningful. Still, the success of any book should not be measured with money but how much it has changed you or made you happy.

Conclusion

Thanks for making it through to the end of this book. I hope it was informative and that it was able to provide you with all of the tools you need to achieve your goals whatever they may be.

The next step is to apply everything that you have learned and start writing your dream book. By now, you should already have the right foundation and understanding of what it means to write a book. As you can see, writing a book is a journey. It can also be a life-changing experience. Indeed, there is so much fun and so many challenges that you will encounter when you write a book.

Books have always been a part of our culture. Writing a book immortalizes anything. By following the lessons in this manual, you will write and finish your book. However, you should keep in mind that having knowledge alone is not enough. You should also take the right actions to actually write your book and turn your dream into a reality.

So, now you know how to write a book. It is up to you to take action and actually start writing your book. Of course, you should start it as soon as possible. If you are serious about becoming a writer, then now is the time for you to start writing a book. Stop delaying it for too long. Now is the time to take positive actions and finally put that story or any book to paper and make it last forever.

If you want to have more information about how to write your own book, how to outline your own book or how to self publish a book check out my Amazon Author page where you will find all my guide to help you write and publish your own books.

Finally, if you found this book useful in any way, a review on Amazon is always appreciated!

www.ingramcontent.com/pod-product-compliance
Lightning Source LLC
Chambersburg PA
CBHW061727250726
48657CB00002B/803